MARY EMMERLING'S
AMERICAN COUNTRY
COTTAGES

MARY EMMERLING'S
AMERICAN COUNTRY
COTTAGES

Photographs by Joshua Greene
Text by Carol Sama Sheehan

Design by Adriane Stark

Clarkson Potter/Publishers
New York

To Juanita Jones—

with love for eighteen years and forever

Also by Mary Emmerling

Mary Emmerling's American Country West
Mary Emmerling's American Country Hearts
Mary Emmerling's American Country Classics
Mary Emmerling's American Country Flags
Mary Emmerling's American Country Christmas List Book
Mary Emmerling's American Country Details
Mary Emmerling's New Country Collecting
Mary Emmerling's Quick Decorating

Text copyright © 1993 by Mary Emmerling
Photographs copyright © 1993 by Joshua Greene

Published by Clarkson N. Potter, Inc., 201 East 50th Street, New York, New York 10022. Member of the Crown Publishing Group.

Random House, Inc. New York, Toronto, London, Sydney, Auckland
www.randomhouse.com

CLARKSON N. POTTER, POTTER, and colophon are trademarks of Clarkson N. Potter, Inc.

Printed in China

Library of Congress Cataloging-in-Publication Data
Emmerling, Mary Ellisor
[American country cottages]
Mary Emmerling's American country cottages / photographs by Joshua Greene.
1. Decoration and ornament, Rustic—United States. 2. Cottages—United States. I. Title.
NK2002.E467   1993
728.37′0973—dc20   92–24897

ISBN 0-517-58365-8

8 10 12 14 16 15 13 11 9

Acknowledgments

Cottages have always been my first love, and I loved working on a book of these wonderful, charming houses.

I can't be too far from a beach at any time. As a child, I looked for coins under the boardwalk, swam in the ocean, rode ponies, biked all day, went to the amusement park all night, and of course, ate far too many french fries and saltwater taffy.

Now I spend much of my year in a compound of cottages on the Atlantic Ocean. I am totally at peace at the cottages—in my garden with my summer flowers and vegetables, or with the rabbits in the herb garden, or just reading a good book and talking to the kids and friends on the screened porch. The kids love the freedom at the beach—biking for hours, walking on the beach with our dog, Star (winter is even better for this).

In writing this book, I found that there are lots of people like me who, after being at work in the city all week (or in airports, where I always seem to be), love to come home to small cozy spaces that give more than they demand in return. For helping me enjoy my complex life, I am grateful for my cottage home.

I am also grateful to all the people who share my love of cottage life and contributed their vision to this book: Rosemari Agostini and Doug Marsden, Tom and Claire Callaway, Janey and John Chatfield, Tony Childs, Dian Bethune-Coble and Richard Coble, Barbara Dente, Gep Durenberger, Diane Flynn and Kathleen King, Susan Frame, Lyn and David Kaufelt, Henry Kuryla, Lys Marigold, Richard Martino, Lee Mindel, Mario Montes and Jeremy Switzer, Ellen O'Neill and her daughter Bridget, Donna Russo, Herbie Schinderman, Jan Schoenmaker and Barry Archung, Bob Smith, Emelie Tolley, Laurie Warner and Eddie Garrick, and Peri Wolfman and Charley Gold.

Always to Jonathan and Samantha, who bring love home to me every day.

To my agents, Gayle Benderoff and Deborah Geltman, who are always there for me.

To everyone at Clarkson Potter, but especially Lauren Shakely—a big kiss; Kristin Frederickson; Howard Klein; Joan Denman; Mark McCauslin; the designer, Adriane Stark; Hilary Bass, for all she does for me; and Crown President and Publisher Michelle Sidrane.

To Nancy Novogrod and *HG* for my shoot with Rosemari Agostini and Doug Marsden and Joshua Greene's shoot with my good friends Peri Wolfman and Charley Gold and photographer Chris Mead.

And a special thanks to Tara Icke of Wisconsin; Joshua Greene, for another beautiful book and for not minding (or not telling me he minds) stopping on the road for another shot; Gloria List, a special friend, for all her help opening up the doors and friendships in California; and, of course, Carol Sheehan, whose inimitable style always helps me say just what I want to.

Mary Emmerling

CONTENTS

INTRODUCTION

first came upon the four modest beach rentals that would become my ideal of cottage living several years ago, on the way to a beach in Sagaponack, New York. The tiny one-floor buildings, perched on concrete blocks like wading birds in a sea of grass, were located on the lee side of the barrier dune that protects the eastern tip of Long Island from the Atlantic Ocean.

At the time, the rentals were occupied by strangers, summer people who came and went in search of tans. Yet the structures themselves, with their chimneys, shingle siding, and makeshift porches, looked like old friends gathered for a reunion. They gave the distinct impression of belonging together.

In this humble compound I saw a chance to reconstruct the elements of the summer houses that had marked the sunny days of my childhood. In doing so, I rediscovered the unique appeal of life in a cottage, no matter which of many forms it happens to take, and the simple pleasures, unpretentious comforts, and abiding romance such a life affords. Now that so many of us find ourselves living in smaller spaces, at least for part of each year, the cottage also seems to offer lessons about what is truly important to us.

When I was a girl, my family, settled in Washington, D.C., spent summers in Rehoboth and Bethany Beach, two classic beach-and-boardwalk towns on the Delaware coast. The house we would take invariably had a screened-in porch, tumbledown rooms with bare wood floors, and the lived-in look that comes from two kids running in and out all day.

For me, summer was an idyllic time of collecting shells in shoe boxes, playing card

games on rainy days, helping with crab boils and cookouts, sleeping under crisp white sheets, and sweeping the sand out of the house on Sunday night before we climbed into the car for the trip home. The values, traditions, and unexpected joys of so simple an existence taught me the positive influence of a dwelling where people, not objects, come first, and where sentiment is the substance.

Webster defines "cottage" as a small one-story house, but many of the buildings that fit the description lack the intrinsic charm of what we think of as a cottage. My definition includes some other characteristics:

• All cottages are small, but as architect Christopher Alexander observes, "Small size does not preclude richness of form." His description in *A Pattern Language* stresses the informal and cozy nature of the cottage floor plan, which permits a "generosity of movement," a minimum of doors and corridors, and "a central space, with nooks around it" for conversation, intimacy, meditation, and contemplation of nature.

• All cottages are linked to their natural surroundings in ways that mere "houses" often are not. A suburban house may seem isolated from the earthly world by its manicured lawn and shrubbery, but the cottage exalts nature through its windows and porches, and becomes an organic part of it with rambling terraces, patios, and gardens.

• All cottages are compact and cozy. They are scaled to simple human needs and the honest values associated with country life

among good friends and family. The word "snug," synonymous with cottage life, comes to us from the Dutch, whose seafaring traditions showed up in their economical use of space in home design. Narrow staircases and beds built into walls were elements found both on the ships and in the houses of the Dutch.

"As every homemaker knows," writes Witold Rybczynski in *Home*, "the less furniture there is, the easier it is to keep a room clean, and this too may have had some-

thing to do with the relative sparseness of the Dutch interior, for these houses were spotlessly, immaculately, unbelievably clean." Like the 17th-century Dutch householder, today's cottage dweller keeps his possessions shipshape by necessity and preference.

• All cottages fully exploit their limited space. The kitchen is generally a communal room where everyone gathers not just to

prepare and enjoy food but to socialize and relax. The room with the hearth, whether fireplace or wood stove, is the focal point for conversation and entertaining. The bedroom is a serene and restful retreat. The omnipresent porch serves as an outdoor room for lounging, dining, napping, and stowing odds and ends in transit.

The real magic of cottage living lies in its simplicity and romance. Most of us formed our earliest impressions of cottages from fairy tales. The cottage in the forest was an idiosyncratic house with a thatched roof, tiny windows, a crooked chimney, and a Dutch door offering a peek into the world of fantasy.

In reality, cottages do offer some of the comfortable pleasures of make-believe. Agatha Christie fans always feel at home in the rose-covered cottage of Miss Marple. The "nest of comforts" of Jane Austen's *Mansfield Park* heroine was a cottager's dream:

"Her plants, her books—of which she had been a collector from the first hour of her commanding a shilling—her writing desk, and her works of charity and ingenuity, were all within her reach . . . she could scarcely see an object in that room which had not an interesting remembrance connected with it."

Both the Cotswold cottage of southern

England and the Norman cottage of the French countryside became powerful models of the ideal small country habitat, and their many virtues quickly spread to other cultures through books, magazines, and movies. *The Enchanted Cottage*, a three-hanky 1945 film starring Robert Young and Dorothy McGuire, epitomized the cottage's enduring appeal as a place where miracles happen. When the battle-scarred veteran falls in love with the painfully plain servant girl, we know

a quaint rustic cottage has cast its spell once again.

The Cape Cod cottage, appearing around 1815, was the first cottage form in America. A diminutive form of the Cape Cod house, it came with a keeping room and kitchen garden and was often surrounded with lilacs, wisteria, and roses. Like most of today's cottages, it was a place where the back door was the true portal, and no one except the minister came around to the front.

Two styles that came along later in the 19th century also proved eminently adaptable to the cottage form.

The Queen Anne style, commonly found in coastal towns along the Eastern Seaboard, harked back to Colonial architecture but had a Victorian twist. Houses were clad with patterned shingles and endowed with picturesque features such as rambling porches, bay windows, sheltered balconies, window seats, and inglenooks. When the popular style was adapted for the smaller cottage, many of these features were retained.

The bungalow, first built in this country in the 1880s, originated in India as a British adaptation of a local style known as "bangla," and served as guest lodgings for visiting officials of the Empire. Bungalows, usually one or one and a half stories in height, are often characterized by pleasant front porches, an open floor plan, and the use of natural textures and colors.

"The bungalow appealed to both middle-class and working-class home owners," observed historian Thomas J. Schlereth in *Victorian America*, 1991; he also noted that the small-house form transcended geo-

graphical as well as class lines: "Construction materials varied according to the region: stucco and redwood on the Pacific coast, adobe in the Southwest, red brick in Midwest cities, board-and-batten in the South, and cobblestone and clapboard in the Northeast."

With their field-stone fireplaces and grape arbors, bungalows had a distinct bucolic flavor that made them suitable to almost any landscape. Clair Baisly, author of *Cape Cod Architecture*, 1989, notes, "They were happy in the hills, lovely at the lake and successful at the seashore."

The cottage is so appealing for our time because it is easy to live in, easy to furnish, easy to maintain, and easy to adapt to every season. Utility and economy govern the plan of the cottage, and were responsible for its popularity at the turn of the century, when life in industrialized urban areas of America first began to pall. "The chief value of these little houses," wrote a contributor to *The Craftsman* magazine in 1904, "lies in the fact that although they are but the simplest of cottages, they nevertheless possess a beauty and individuality which is lacking in many a residence that costs ten times as much."

A cottage does not put on airs, but its rudimentary architecture and country setting endow it with an authentic charm. Every cottage has its own personality, never brash, never calling attention to itself, never pretending to be something it is not. "The useful should never be sacrificed to the ornamental" was one of the dictates, still applicable today, of the 19th-century American landscape architect and cottage proponent A. J. Downing. The informal layout of a cottage invites intimacy in the way that the unstudied design of a cottage garden encourages

relaxation, reminiscence, and contemplation.

There are cottages and then there are cottages. In Great Britain, the first of the form were small rural shelters for peasants, not much more elaborate than improvised huts. In the United States, the Newport "cottage" built for Cornelius Vanderbilt in 1892 had seventy rooms and a gilded Renaissance great hall complete with crystal chandeliers and torchères.

In *American Country Cottages*, buildings as varied in appearance as a Yankee-plain farmhouse in New England and a Spanish Colonial bungalow in California function as cottages. Cottage interiors, which by their intimacy encourage the expression of individual taste, are also wildly different: a seaside cottage full of nautical collections, a Victorian confection with floral accents, an all-white room with two or three pieces of furniture. Cottages may start life as boathouses, sheds, or other mundane outbuildings before un-

dergoing miraculous conversions. My own cottages—four of them comprising a communal compound—offer yet another variation, demonstrating how a few tiny structures can be made to serve as a single cottage with a multiple personality.

In some ways, the cottage is more a state of mind and a life-style than a set of physical characteristics. "As anyone who has ever lived in a cottage will attest," notes Richard Sexton, who has specialized in documenting cottages in the San Francisco Bay area, "there is something about them—their intimacy, coziness, or maybe their unabashed goofiness—that enraptures their occupants in a special way."

In my experience as both homeowner and renter, I have lived in a city loft, above a store, in apartments of one bedroom, and in apartments with "house"-size rooms. I have renovated an antique farmhouse, built a new farmhouse to look like an antique, and fallen head-over-heels for a conch-house cottage in Key West, Florida. But all along the way, my family's summer cottage remained the touchstone of how to make a home—cozy, comfortable, and accommodating of family and friends and their comings and goings. So, in my remake of the cottage compound I discovered by the sea, I have come full circle in my understanding of what a home should be.

When E. M. Forster described the redbrick cottage of his 1910 novel *Howards End*, he put into words all that a cottage really means: "It is old and little, and altogether delightful."

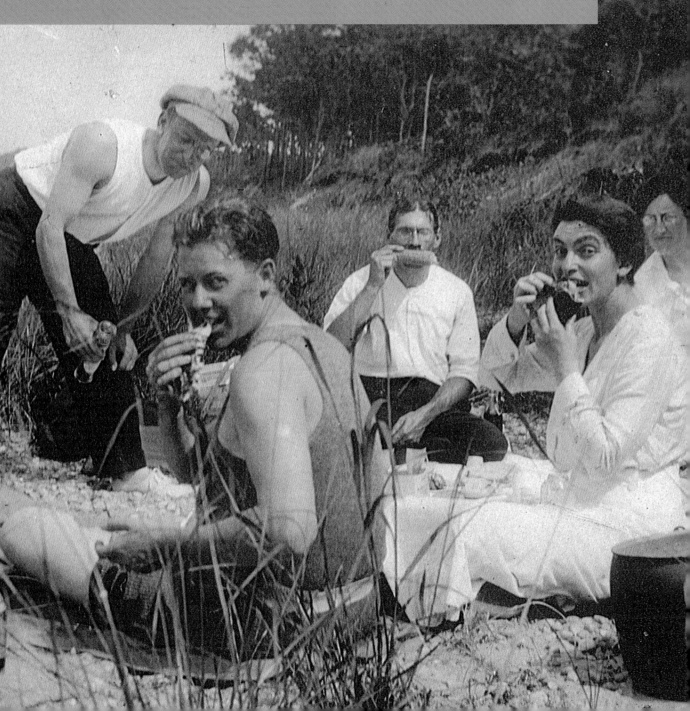

The cottage by the sea is America's classic summer getaway. Of course, the time is past when families routinely packed up and left town on the last day of school to spend uninterrupted months at the shore, not to return home until after Labor Day. But the appeal of a lazy summer of freedom and all the idle pleasures that cottage life has to offer continues. Anyone who has ever spent more than a day in a beach cottage has a vivid sensory recollection of the experience— the smell of salt air and wild roses, the feel of an ocean breeze on your face, and the self-indulgent sensation of sitting down on a rattan sofa in your wet bathing suit. A beachcomber philosophy allows the cottage to take on any guise so long as it makes few demands on the cottager. There may be precious possessions back in town, but time is the priceless commodity of a cottage by the sea.

*On pristine Georgica Pond,
summer revolves around the
traditional pastimes of sailing,
gardening, and reading.*

HOME WITH A PEDIGREE

Dogs, dogs, everywhere you look," is how Lys Marigold sums up her approach to creating a cottage look with a distinctive pedigree. The traditional Long Island cottage, parts of which date to the 17th century, owes its unique personality to Lys's collection of canine memorabilia, from andirons to oil portraits, not to mention her toy spaniel. "I've had a lot of fun putting the collection together," she notes. "However, in a cottage this size, you really have to make a place for something before you bring it home." An avid gardener ("The name 'Marigold' helped," she says), Lys has surrounded her cottage with pink 'Maiden's Blush' roses climbing the picket fence, old-fashioned cottage perennials, and a culinary herb garden including "Corsican mint that smells like crème de menthe when you rub your thumb over it."

ABOVE: *French country lace curtain with swan motif. Broods of cygnets, ospreys, cormorants, piping plover, egrets, and herons are born every spring near the pond and in the surrounding marshes.* LEFT: *A collection of French and English dog paintings echoes the playful canine theme throughout the cottage.* RIGHT: *The front of the house, with its gambrel roof, cedar shakes, and fanlight-topped door, evokes an English country cottage; the pond side, with its dark shingles, tall pines, and dock, suggests a camp in the Adirondacks.*

OPPOSITE: *Staffordshire spaniels and Brussels Griffons occupy the place of honor on the mantel; chintz-covered and wicker chairs provide comfort for humans.*

LEFT: *Georgica Rose, the English toy spaniel named after the pond, finds a spot in the dining room under* **The Frozen Pond** *by Bruce Crane, who painted in East Hampton in the 1880s.* ABOVE: *A cottage-size table suits the dining room, as does the built-in corner cupboard, original to the house, in which a collection of Danish sea-gull-pattern china evokes the cottage's beach location.*

NEW ENGLAND CLASSIC

I love the wild charm of the place," says the owner of this cottage, which overlooks a pond teeming with waterfowl and three acres of wild grassy marsh, informal gardens, and a sprawling lawn. Thousands of naturalized daffodils and tulips announce the arrival of spring, and the splendor of the garden continues throughout the year. "The only flowers we bring into the cottage are the ones we grow ourselves," she says. Her taste for English and American antiques finds expression in the cottage itself. A

24

*On a saltwater pond, the passing
parade of country life and the
bounty of a summer garden are
enjoyed from Adirondack chairs.*

PRECEDING PAGES, LEFT: *The mudroom remains a bright spot in the cottage, with a deacon's bench painted cobalt blue and fishing tackle at the ready.* PRECEDING PAGES, RIGHT: *In the living room, an English pine mirror hangs above a trestle table trimmed at the corners into an oval shape. Crockery brimming with dried flowers signals a new season.* ABOVE: *Two checked wing chairs flank the mantel in the living room.*

descendant of a 19th-century British prime minister, she is naturally drawn to the traditions of English country life, which suit the landscape and style of the New England seacoast cottage she shares with her husband and teenage daughter. Although "falling down when we bought it," the cottage with its storybook appeal quickly won over the family. "We didn't want to touch anything." The original

LEFT: *The mullioned window, one of the hallmarks of cottage style, is picture-window size in this dining room simply furnished with an American harvest table and English pine country chairs.*
ABOVE: *The cottage grounds feature classic picket fences and abundant gardens.*

ABOVE: *Favorite summer pastimes are memorialized with a model sloop and a collection of local seashells.* BELOW: *A twig settee emblazoned with stars and a rustic table make the flower garden into an outdoor room.*

ABOVE: *In a cottage where space is at a premium, an English plate rack, standing on the floor instead of mounted on the wall, stores an assortment of treasured antique dishes and platters, and shows them off at the same time.*

woodwork makes an authentic backdrop for the pine furniture, the blue-and-white china from England, and the rustic American pieces. Although two careers require the couple to spend their weekdays in town, this is not just a summer retreat. Her husband, whose passion for sailing finds an outlet on nearby Long Island Sound, "never wants to wake up on Sunday morning and not be here," she declares. "Every weekend when I walk through the cottage, its old-fashioned and authentic feeling gives me a strong sense of belonging."

RIGHT: *Hand-hewn beams and boards provide a rustic passageway to the new master bedroom, where a recent painting pays tribute to a neighborhood landmark.*

A GARDENER'S COTTAGE

Some cottages must be rescued from the mistakes of the past. That's what happened with this shingled beach cottage, originally built in the 1920s. When the new owners discovered it, the cottage had imitation stucco walls and an unattractive boulder-rock fireplace. The interior was gutted to create a freer flow among the rooms. The fireplace was rebuilt with old brick and an 1840 pine mantel located in

Bouquets, screen doors, and weather-beaten shingles lend an aura of charm to a traditional seaside cottage from the 1920s. Boxwood shrubs flanking the front entry thrive, with a yearly trim, in the moist ocean air.

ABOVE: *A pine chest of drawers stores linens and towels, giving the bathroom a rustic feeling. An antique blanket rack holds towels for everyday use. The warm light of a stately little table lamp replaces fluorescent glare.*

RIGHT: *The unexpected contrast of a polished wood ball and flowering vine provides a small-scale drama for the eye.* BELOW: *An old iron bed painted black and dressed in white provides cool refuge in the heat of summer.*

ABOVE: *A picketed railing is a whimsical note at the back of the cottage, where the garage doubles as a garden shed and laundry room. The two-wheeler is the fuel-efficient transportation to the shore or village. The cottagers, devoted gardeners, have added plantings appropriate to the setting, a private cul-de-sac in a neighborhood established in the 1920s. "Everything is rather simple and old-fashioned," says one of the owners.*

FOLLOWING PAGES: *Awash in sunlight, this beach cottage keeps furnishings and fuss to a minimum. A pair of fish decoys carved in the American Northeast perches atop an English pine blanket chest.*

a salvage yard. Through the owners' own gardening efforts, inspired by a four-year stay in England, the rooms are filled with blooms of delphinium, hydrangea, 'New Dawn' roses, Montauk daisies, and a host of white, pink, and blue annuals from the cutting garden. But apart from the profusion of flowers and herbs, this is a pared-down English cottage. "I've always had eclectic tastes and love to mix periods, countries, patterns," says one of the owners. She used English chintz cushions for antique wicker chairs and dressed an overstuffed sofa and a pair of club chairs in loose-fitting slipcovers. "Usually, your eye is true, so if you buy what you like, it will work with everything else you like."

OPPOSITE: *A well-appointed dining porch can be the heart of cottage living. Under the blustery gaze of Aeolus on a salvaged frieze, the owners placed a table fashioned from century-old floorboards and an antique trestle base.*

CLOCKWISE FROM LEFT: *Floral chintz on a Biedermeier stool, a pitcher of flowers on a bench with a shell motif, and dried roses on a demilune table.*

ANTIQUE
SALTBOX

Dating from the 1830s, this cottage near Acabonic Harbor was once a humble outbuilding on one of the oldest estates on eastern Long Island. Asa Miller, an early settler of the historic Springs area of East Hampton and the estate's original owner, may have had the cedar-shingle saltbox built as quarters for his gardener. Although the briny air of the nearby ocean wafts through the grounds, especially in summer, the cottage has a distinct bucolic presence, with established beds of irises, daylilies, flowering clematis, and hydrangea. It has been brought back to life in the tradition of its time and place by Susan Frame, a New York City

A vine-covered former gardener's cottage on an old estate retains its inimitable connection to the natural world with twig furniture, an equestrian weather vane from the turn of the century, flowers from the cutting garden, and a lofty home for purple martins.

psychologist and passionate collector of Americana. "Things aren't perfect in cottages of this age—the floor slants, and my tallest visitors have to duck through some of the doorways," she observes. "But what you might lose in space you gain in coziness." Hand-hewn beams, wide pine floorboards, wainscoting, and hand-blown eight-light windows give the cottage a rustic character that enhances its charm, and Susan has highlighted the natural virtues of her home with her choice of furnishings. She scoured the surrounding villages for pieces

TOP: *Irregular wide-plank pine flooring lends warmth to the living room.* ABOVE: *Fresh flowers brighten nearly every room.*

LEFT: *Panels of a venerable Hoosier cabinet lighten the load of the housewife of the day with such aids as a cookbook holder and a dial-a-staple list.* ABOVE: *Sliding doors bring abundant light into the cottage.*

Exposing hand-hewn beams opened up the living room, permitting the creation of a sleeping loft. A library ladder provides access to the loft and the collection of books and old bottles.

ABOVE: *The typical narrow cottage kitchen often requires the use of open shelving and other storage tricks. A disciplined pick-up-and-put-away approach keeps surfaces neat; baskets and old canning jars used for storage are attractive as well as practical.*

ABOVE: *The nondigital world of the cottage is captured in the pure lines of a hand-painted Connecticut-made clock from the 1880s.* RIGHT: *First made in the 1920s to accommodate the growing modernization of the American kitchen, Hoosier cabinets lend themselves to the unpretentious catchall quality of cottage living.*

that reflect authentic local seafaring and agricultural traditions, such as an enormous needle once used for mending fishnets, now on the dining room wall, and an array of farming implements displayed over the brick hearth. Even so homely an object as an old cuspidor fits into the cottage—as a handy container for potpourri.

ABOVE: *This cottage dweller draws on her collection of textiles to soften and enliven every room. In her diminutive master bedroom, she maximizes space, using stools as nightstands and wall-mounted fixtures.*
LEFT: *The Victorian ladder-back chair comes in handy as a valet.*

A utility company's discarded cable spool and an Italian market umbrella are the basic elements of an outdoor dining room. (PHOTO: CHRIS MEAD)

SMALL WONDER

Cottages and herb gardens have been closely associated for centuries, so it's no surprise that Emelie Tolley, a leading author on herbs (*Herbs, Gifts from the Herb Garden*), would find herself a getaway that combines the best of both. Nostalgic for her childhood summers, "when all I had to think about was which books to curl up with," Emelie saw in a neglected beach shack a chance to recapture those sunnier times. With so much of her year devoted to travel and research for her books, Emelie was attracted to the idea of the simplified social life that a tiny country rental offered. "As much as

ABOUT: *A tiny screened entry has room for the portable bar in its milkman's carrier.* OPPOSITE: *In an unfinished wall, trim shelves store enamelware finds above a makeshift drop-leaf serving board.*

ABOVE: *Improvisation is the key to furnishing a rental cottage. A chest of drawers becomes a decorative table with a tailored skirt (attached with Velcro) and a plaid linen tablecloth.* RIGHT: *Twin guest beds double as sofas with piqué slipcovers and frilly pillow shams.*

one-room living forces you to be neat," she wryly observes, "it also eliminates the prospect of wave after wave of house-guests." The limited space has not cramped her enthusiasm for entertaining, though. "I've had as many as ten friends here for dinner," she says, "and I can even make room for the occasional overnight guest as well." Double-duty furniture makes it possible to sleep, eat, and entertain in one room. Portable furnishings expand her horizons into the yard and garden. Like English workers' cottage gardens, Emelie's backyard plot allows her to season menus and create natural decorations. "Even the smallest of herb gardens," she observes, "can be a place of enchantment."

ABOVE: *In the backyard, Emelie has room for plots of flowers, herbs, and summer vegetables, assuring a full season's supply of fresh ingredients for a gardener who loves to cook.*

OPPOSITE: *A rustic bowl filled with sea lavender, a wicker tray strewn with petals, and a pitcher full of Queen Anne's lace and cosmos bring the simple glories of the summer indoors.* LEFT: *The shower, original to the 1930s cottage, offers the basic comforts of a rustic spa.*

SHED WITH A VIEW

When you walk up, you expect to throw the doors wide open and find a tractor parked inside," says Bob Smith about his farm shed turned summer cottage. Instead, there's an inviting bar and a curtained bed. A rudimentary structure that was originally part of a large farm complex, Bob's one-room shed has the ambience and appurtenances of a full-fledged beach cottage. "I wanted to retain a farmhouse character, so I left the chestnut beams and barn boards ex-

With its picket fence and rose-draped arbor, this former farm shed becomes a genuine cottage, hung with "an oddball collection of seascape paintings by local amateur artists."

53

posed," says Bob about the relatively simple reclamation project he undertook five years ago. He stripped off the tarpaper siding, restored the cedar shakes on the exterior, and then painted the cement floor gray to match the weathered wood. Inside, he surrounded himself with things that were visually delightful, "but nothing pretentious." With its proximity to the ocean, its flowering trees and bushes, a perennial garden, and "a sea of pink roses," Bob's cottage is nevertheless his castle, at least for the summer.

LEFT: *Furnishings for the simple one-room building are homelike and plain—recycled rattan furniture, an old oak chest, a Portuguese rug, and various pictures and other oddments—nothing of special value but all "visually delightful and pleasing."*

Open to the natural world on all sides, the cottage outgrows its structural dimensions.

An improvised peg rack high on the exposed barn boards of the shed adds colorful storage.

Vines are the magicians of nature, concealing exterior walls while shielding the neighbors' view. Resplendent throughout the year in a riot of native color, the courtyard of this southern California seaside cottage makes a welcoming oasis for friends, felines, and birds alike, with charming reminders of blooms to come staked in the ground.

PACIFIC PEARL

I have always loved flowers and wanted to have them at all times of the year. So I try to have something blooming in every season," says Janet Chatfield. In the process of teaching herself to garden, Janet created a little piece of paradise on a bluff overlooking the Pacific Ocean. She occupies one of five tiny cottages originally built in 1948 as seasonal rentals for patrons of the legendary Del Mar racetrack. Access to the out-of-doors and ingenious use of her collections and storage space in the 420-square-foot interior make the cottage feel spacious.

THIS PAGE: *The spectacular eight-mile-wide view of the Pacific eliminates any chance of claustrophobia in a tiny cottage.* OPPOSITE: *The window seat on the patio overlooking the bluff provides vantage points for enjoying a panoramic view. The verdant courtyard makes picnicking a special occasion in all seasons.*

SHIP ON SHORE

Anchored by dunes on one side and potato fields on the other, this simple shingle-clad cottage of the beach-shack variety puts on no airs, except for those provided courtesy of the Atlantic Ocean. For the Schindermans, renting a cottage at the beach is a way of forcing themselves to adopt an uncomplicated way of life. "The great appeal of this place is its low-key, casual way," says Herbie Schinderman. Both Herbie, an antiques importer, and his wife, Donna, vice-president of publicity for Warner Records, are in constant motion, traveling on behalf of business and among homes as far-flung as a ranch in Wyoming and a country house in Scotland (the base of buying operations for his business, Ann-Morris, Inc.). Seeking to strike a balance be-

As breezy as a ride in a vintage Cadillac convertible, an unadorned beach cottage perched upon the dunes gives a family with young children a summer's respite.

tween the demands of their hectic careers and the desire to spend quiet time with their young children, they saw in this beach rental a route to the simple life they craved. "The house is unique because it doesn't make any demands," says Herbie. "In a way, it's like going to summer camp, where everything is there for you."

The cottage is actually two that have been connected. The renovation borrowed some of the space-saving measures perfected by boatwrights. "There are a lot of built-ins," explains Herbie, "so we didn't have to bring much with us: just a few pieces of furniture to make things comfortable."

LEFT: *The built-in eating table and benches, with stow area above, comprise a landlocked version of a ship's galley.* ABOVE: *In the living room, the river-rock hearth makes its sturdy presence felt against cedar-clad walls.*

ABOVE: *Yeomanly furnishings suit the basic needs.* LEFT AND ABOVE RIGHT: *A ladder allows a deck and rooftop observation point to be used for sun-bathing.* RIGHT: *Hooks and built-ins make a teak bathroom shipshape.*

A master bedroom is transformed into a sleeping porch via a dreamy
canopy of mosquito netting. A bank of windows is nature's air-
conditioning. Marseilles spreads unite the cottage's odds and ends.

COMMUNAL LIVING

The Kennedy compound, the famous Cape Cod retreat where the First Family sailed, threw clambakes, and played a fierce game of touch football in the 1960s, memorably expressed the idea of being together as a clan. In fact, compounds at the shore, on the lake, or in the woods have long served as family retreats. The great camps of the Adirondacks, first built in the 1880s, were clusters of cabins where guests came and went all summer long, free to socialize and just as free to be on their own. The cottage compound offers the same versatility and flexibility on a more intimate scale. One cottage usually serves as headquarters, but there may also be a dining pavilion, a pool house, a studio, guest quarters, or a summer kitchen to augment the little community; a garden, almost invariably, is the central campus. Today's compounds, which often take in adjoining properties, former outbuildings, or even the guest cabins of an abandoned motel, offer the same combination of privacy and togetherness that inspired the compound tradition.

KEY WEST CONCH

Not all cottage gardens are created equal. In the Solaris Hill neighborhood of Key West (designated "Hill" because it is all of eighteen feet above sea level), the tropical version of the pinks, blues, and whites at England's Sissinghurst may be found in the compound of two garden designers, Jan Schoenmaker and Barry Archung. Making use of their collection of native and rare palms and orchids from Asia and tropical America, they have filled a unique place with the colors and foliage of a rain forest. A towering avocado tree shades the pool and is a host to dozens of orchids in a range of torrid hues. No vegetation could be more compatible with a cottage of hard southern pine and cypress constructed by local boat builders 130 years

Located on one of the smallest parcels of land in Key West, this 1860 conch house makes up, along with a cookhouse, a tropics-style compound.

LEFT AND RIGHT:
*A well-stocked
cookhouse kitchen
overlooks the com-
pound's sun deck
and dipping pool.*

ABOVE AND LEFT:
*A tiny bathroom
has several unusu-
al touches: a deco-
rative old cabin
light fixture, a
mirror retrieved
from a local ship-
wreck, and a
permanent pair of
helping hands.*

ABOVE: *Cultivated orchids, indoors and out, lend sensuous charm to the cottage compound.* BELOW: *High ceilings, six-over-six windows, and pastel colors are island tricks for combating the heat.*

ABOVE: **The Love Quilt,** *by Key West artisan Lucille Kravitz, vividly frames a workstation in the bedroom.* OPPOSITE: *The cot in the guest room is an authentic copy of a Gloucester sea hammock of a century ago.*

ago. The adjacent cookhouse, nearly as old and until recently used as a laundry room and storage shed, has been restored to its original function. (In the Old South, kitchens were often built separately to protect the main house from heat and the danger of fire). The palette of tropical pastel colors for both the interiors and exteriors was chosen to reflect the cottage's Bahamian heritage.

When they made their home in New England, Jan and Barry had lived by the adage "If you don't like the weather, wait five minutes." But while living in Key West, says Jan, "We practice the old island custom—keep the windows and doors closed on the hot side of the house, and let the cool air come in from the other side."

A collection of orchids and rare and unusual palms, both potted and in the ground, provides the deck, walkways, and poolside with lush color and equatorial ambience.

FOUR OF A KIND

Memories of carefree summers spent vacationing with my family on Delaware's Eastern Shore inspired me to convert a group of undistinguished beach rentals into a compound of summer houses. The four single-story dwellings are only a short walk from the ocean and well within shouting distance of one another. They all have screened-in porches and range from a one-roomer to a two-bedroom house; each has its own personality. One is classic beach-style,

An all-American compound of four tiny cottages by the sea is refuge for three generations of Emmerlings, who gather for a summer of country entertaining.

OPPOSITE: *In Hollyhocks Cottage, stacked painted benches become a surprisingly practical bookshelf.* LEFT: *Panels of discarded awning fabric make inexpensive shades for a screened-in porch.*

ABOVE AND RIGHT: *An inveterate collector of seashells and Stars and Stripes, Mary celebrates the Fourth of July all summer long.*

filled with rattan and wicker. Another is southwestern, with rustic furnishings and a cowboys-and-Indians motif. The tiniest is the simplest—almost like a cabin at summer camp. My favorite, and the one I use most often for myself, is unabashedly romantic. Surrounded by a privet hedge, the cottages share a picket-fenced garden of old-fashioned flowers and herbs in a communal lawn, an arrangement that encourages group activities while preserving privacy.

ABOVE: *Even when visitors forget to make their beds, crazy-quilt spreads keep the room inviting.*
RIGHT: *A basket keeps knockabout shoes paired off for impulsive trips to the beach or town—and keeps the sand out of the bedroom.*
FAR RIGHT: *Perched on an old step stool in Mary's bedroom, baskets hold important accessories.*

LEFT: *Space always at a premium in a cottage. Gracefully bracketed open shelves hold the contents of an organized entertainer's china closet.*

BELOW: *Peg racks serve as clothes hangers and closets. A seashell picture frame and kerosene lamps on the bureau recall the beach cottages of the 19th century.*

Stars

ABOVE: *The cottages in the compound surround a central lawn and garden. Each cottage has a screened porch for enjoying the ocean breezes.*

ABOVE: *The porch is the cottage's all-purpose room, suitable for dining, entertaining, or just relaxing. Tea towels fashioned into curtains and a checkered country tablecloth are cottage classics.* RIGHT: *Flower-print-cushioned wicker and a bleached skull from the range make an unexpected combination on True Love Cottage's porch.* OPPOSITE: *In True Love Cottage, furnished camp-style, logs are laid for a cozy fire.*

ABOVE: *A four-drawer unit once used in a general store keeps the silver out of sight; compact task lighting allows the cook to find what she needs.* RIGHT: *Baskets and peg racks help to keep things organized in the bathroom.*

A cottage office features a desk on a pair of old sawhorses painted country blue, a filing cabinet made of wicker, and a milk pail for a wastebasket.

Rose

LEFT: *Patriotic piecework dresses up a pillow and quilt.*
RIGHT: *A community of birdhouses is busy all spring (safe from the cat), then becomes an element of country decor in the summer.*

LEFT: *In the kitchen, a farmhouse table serves as both workstation for the cook and dining table for family and guests.* ABOVE: *Pillows and paintings set a flowery theme in the romantic Rose Cottage.* OPPOSITE: *An antique cupboard offers more storage space than built-in cabinets and has the advantage of mobility.*

The bedroom of Stars Cottage, named after Mary's dog and done up in Western style, celebrates the cowboy tradition with buffalo checks on the bed, cowhide skin on the floor, and a blanket shot through with rootin' tootin' images of the wrangler's trade. A peg rack supplements closet space.

True Love

BELOW: *A duet of chaise longues and a bike at rest represent two of summer's most enduring pleasures.*

ABOVE AND LEFT: *Rustic benches, twig and wicker chairs, and other country furnishings—a cottage's basic ingredients— take on new patterns, colors, and images. Supper for two is served from a narrow table used for books and treasures during daytime hours.*

91

The main house in the compound has a cedar-shingled gable roof like those of the other houses in the neighborhood. Pergolas, one-of-a-kind fixtures, and flowers inside and out establish a friendly cottage atmosphere.

SHINGLED VILLA

The real estate agent kept referring to the property as 'the Dull Estate,'" recalls architect Lee Mindel about the run-down 1920s cottage with the woebegone detached garage that he and his partner, Peter Shelton, have now transformed into a summer retreat. The original house was pieced together with such recycled materials as old telephone poles and salvaged doors. With another associate, Michael Neal, Lee and Peter decided to take apart the jerry-built structure and put it back together. "There's

no question the house went through a major metamorphosis," says Lee. The cluster of three shingled buildings was linked to form a compound "that actually makes my neighbors' houses look like outbuildings of my house." The garage became a guesthouse, and a tiny summer pavilion was erected by the swimming pool. With an ingenious landscape plan that divides the long, narrow front lawn into three progressively smaller areas, the "Dull" site ultimately became a true estate—a miniature version of the grand estates in the area. Linden trees by the street give shade, cherry trees provide privacy, and roses, Montauk daisies, and other perennials offer an endless summer of garden beauty.

LEFT: *The wicker table in the pavilion shows off a collection of mercury glass and a "junky but arresting" Art Deco mirror. Candlelight dinners here are bathed in the glow of sunburst sconces created by London designer André Dubreuil.* BELOW: *The passageway between the pavilion and the main residence was formerly a shared driveway that delineated one boundary of the narrow lot.*

OPPOSITE: *Reminiscent of a Swedish summer house, the pool pavilion has exposed sheathing and framing, and is furnished with flea-market finds and prints of French furniture.*

ABOVE: *An elegant but informal hand brings together such disparate elements as brass lamps from the 1940s, an English tapestry sofa, and, flanking the window, a pair of the first tax maps of Southampton, New York (part of a collection of fifteen), displayed above birch plywood paneling.*

OPPOSITE: *The Baltic pedestal satinwood table and the painted mirror, a relic from an English boarding school, add an unexpected Gothic touch. The king-size cornice crowning the wall provides drawer space for the guest loft on the other side.*

ABOVE: *The curved arms of a late-19th-century French chair and the delicate bow of an upholstered gilt bench are lyrical additions to the guesthouse living room. An Italian surrealist drawing from the 1950s rests on the floor.*

ABOVE: *Gothic arches and original glazing distinguish this mahogany secretary from the Federal period. Among the bibelots is a gold-plated flacon from the 19th century, once used to hold talcum powder.*

BELOW: *Walls painted the color of the sky and a pitcher full of blooms bring the outdoors to the guest bedroom, where bead-center-bead paneling and a crocheted coverlet on a French sleigh bed from 1840 create a relaxed look.* RIGHT: *Dormer windows provide space for sleep as well as light for lazy summer reading.*

"GEP'S FOLIE"

A Mediterranean-style cottage dating from 1926 is the heart of a romantic half acre that also includes a whimsical guesthouse, a pool yard, and a luxurious garden. "Folie Gep" is what G. R. "Gep" Durenberger, an antiques dealer, calls his compound in the middle of a busy southern California beach town, and visitors invariably fall in love with Gep's brand of foolishness. Inside, he has created an enchanting

Spanish tiles, old doors, European antiquities, and the lush plant life of the southern California climate commingle in this idyllic vision of cottage life conceived by a collector and environmentalist whose love of the past is matched by his concern for the future.

LEFT: *The cottage's only surviving window, Gothicized, frames a verdant courtyard. Inside, the Italian Louis XIII table shows off a Dutch canal scene painted on layers of glass, an example of vue optique, the original 3-D art.*

LEFT: *Hedges beyond the window allow for garden views and privacy.*

atmosphere with his collection of 17th- and 18th-century English and European art and furnishings he began acquiring over thirty years ago. "To me," Gep says, "collecting adds to life depth and historical perspective, humor—delight in people past and present—and concern for those to come who may be deprived of enjoying their heritage." In tending his tiny corner of the original property, Gep has preserved the legacy of casual elegance that defined the beach colonies of a younger California.

RIGHT: *Light floods into the living room and across the parquet floor through an arched and dramatically draped alcove window.* LEFT: *Under the fan windows in the entry is a handsome display of 18th-century Marseilles faïence.*

The gardens and grounds surrounding the main cottage and guesthouse were designed, according to the owner, to provide "privacy, self-contained views, reasons to ramble, places in both the sun and the shade, and comfortable perches on which to read, entertain, or just be alone."

LEFT: *At the fanciful geometric window, dishes are left to dry in an antique wire basket.* BELOW: **The dining room boasts Anglo-Indian painted armchairs, an 18th-century French fruitwood commode surmounted by a baroque mirror, and a carved servant from the 17th century.**

LEFT: *A banquette piled with pillows covered with inexpensive hand-blocked cotton and bolsters in vintage French fabric provides built-in seating for dinner guests. The sunburst mirror, a handcraft from Mexico, was inherited with the cottage.* BELOW: *The tool shed, expanded by the owner, serves as a dining pavilion for casual meals.*

ABOVE: *A swag of antique fabric along the handrail turns a set of plain cottage stairs into a platform.*

RIGHT: *A pedimented mirror adds its monumental sweep to a tiny bathroom.*
BELOW: *An antique French pine icebox provides storage. The chair is in the Gothic style.*

OPPOSITE: *Guaranteed to induce pleasant dreams, this sleeping alcove (formerly the garage)—with its 17th-century leaded-pane window, coverlet crocheted by a favorite cousin, and French linen bed curtains—illustrates the magical effects of cottage life.*

DREAM
RANCHO

Midwesterner Thomas Callaway became fasci-
nated with the West as a boy, and when he moved to
California with his wife, Claire, an actress, he was
immediately taken with "the horizontal openness of
Los Angeles and all the Spanish street names." He
purchased a vintage stucco bungalow, virtually un-
touched since it was built in the 1920s, and was
pleased to find on his property the ruins of an

*A columned portal added to a California bungalow provides a platform for
enjoying the courtyard. The windows were distressed by the owner to look as
old as the* trastero *(cupboard) found in a New Mexico adobe.*

ABOVE: *The guest quarters enjoy a sweeping view of the courtyard and the expanse of roof tiles made in Saltillo, Mexico.* ABOVE RIGHT: *Antique tiles from Pueblo, Mexico, grace a fountain wall.* RIGHT: *Visitors are greeted by a pair of old doors with inset peepholes and an ironwood window and grille, over 250 years old.* OPPOSITE: *Adjoining the bungalow is the design studio and guest room with its own balcony. In keeping with the untamed character of the plantings, grass intrudes randomly through the stone coping.*

adobe wall dating from the time of the Spanish land grants. Tom, an actor–decorator–furniture designer, knew he'd found the starting point for his "dream rancho, an Early Spanish Colonial layout with the craftsmanship and detailing that would have been found in the home of an early viceroy or governor." He built a portal (a Spanish veranda) for the 1,000-square-foot bungalow, replaced a decrepit barn with quarters for a studio and guest room, and introduced three small but lush courtyards. A patient perfectionist, Tom added over the years beamed wood ceilings, thick plaster walls and antique doors, more windows, window grilles, and even adobe bricks he made himself from backyard mud.

ABOVE: *William Randolph Hearst acquired the 17th-century Spanish grille on this studio window for San Simeon, but never had it installed.* OPPOSITE: *Kachina dolls on a Navaho woman's wearing blanket, and a Cheyenne cradleboard inscribed with the names of babies from several generations bring an unexpected serenity to a colorful living room.*

ABOVE: *Saws and tools once used by Claire's father and his relatives make a display that is as intriguing as it is useful.*

OPPOSITE: *A fanciful tableau on the old Mexican worktable includes a Spanish Colonial travel chest and a pair of miniature chairs that once served as salesman's samples. The chair was designed by Callaway for his current furniture line.* ABOVE AND RIGHT: *The studio, reached through Dutch doors built by the owner, reflects his eclectic collector's eye in a cabinet top crammed with old books, paintings, and carved figures from Bolivia.*

OPPOSITE: *The ceiling in the guest bedroom was made from old fence boards.* ABOVE: *Native American beadwork adorns Tom Callaway's son Catlin's bedroom wall.*

ABOVE: *A Wisconsin cupboard holds Midwestern folk art and memorabilia, including a mess of fish decoys.* LEFT: *Inset tiles in the child's room were painted and fired by the owner as his version of the trading-post tiles sold to tourists.*

The most rarefied form of cottage life is found in dwellings where less is more, in cottages that radiate their warmth through purity of architecture, the crisp whites of summer linens, and subtleties that are sensed rather than observed. Such cottages hark back to the summer house of yesteryear, with its unadorned walls, bare floors, muslin slipcovers, and windows left uncurtained, the better to drink in views of sand and sky. "My cottage is like a stage setting for any production, it's so understated," one owner observes, yet each of these cottages is markedly unique. One evokes the restrained elegance of a Scandinavian fjord house. Another shows its roots as a family farmstead. Yet another remains faithful to the Spanish Colonial legacy of early California. Deceptively simple, these cottages offer a refuge for busy lives.

HOLLYWOOD HAVEN

With dreamy rooms awash in faded rose, gossamer sheers, and the glimmer of gilt-encrusted furnishings, all against a dazzling ivory background, a cottage built in 1924 has been infused with the magic and mystery of the golden age of Hollywood, when Rudolph Valentino and Gloria Swanson set the standard for glamour. "I tried to restore the cottage as close as possible to its original condition," says pro-

From the decorative ironwork that tops an arched window in the living room to the red tile that crowns the roof, Hollywood's past lives on in a 1924 cottage. Architectural fragments lend character to its patio garden.

fessional makeup artist Dian Bethune-Coble, "while expanding upon and enhancing its elegant Spanish character." She put down tiles from Saltillo, Mexico, on exterior stairs and patios, replaced louvered windows with light-spreading panes, and added classic stenciling to floors and ceilings. Ivory walls and white slipcovers and curtains, bathed in natural light, set off painted furniture, exotically patterned rugs, and period decorative work.

Although her property is small, Dian worked with a landscape designer to turn her backyard into "as wonderful and tranquil an area as possible," planting bougainvillea, native palms, camellias, bottle brush trees, ivy, roses, and calla lilies.

OPPOSITE: *The grand style of Mediterranean Spain is most evident in the Roman arches, hand-painted tiles, and grillwork that embellish the stucco façade.* ABOVE: *In the entry, small furnishings accommodate bonnets and bouquets.* ABOVE RIGHT: *Lush vegetation helps give the cottage its sultry character.* RIGHT: *The cottage features all styles, from a formal French chair to the craftsman built kitchen table and banquette and Monterey hanging lamp.*

ABOVE: *Pillows tied to the back of the bench add a note of style and comfort for dining. Over the decorative mantel is a view of the Hollywood Hills painted by Henry Lovins in the 1930s.* RIGHT: *An old armoire is an extra closet in the guest room and displays Indian pottery and an old watering can.*

LEFT: *In the dining room, a 100-year-old kilim rug brings together reproduction Russian armchairs, a rustic old New Mexican bench, and Chippendale-style chairs with Aubusson tapestry seat cushions.*
BELOW: *Down-filled bedding adds comforting luxury to the master bedroom. The calla lilies from the garden, console table with elaborately scrolled legs, Victorian tapestry on the bed, and gilt-framed mirrors (one with a lavish pediment) on facing walls convey the legendary romance of Hollywood.*

THE SIMPLE
LIFE

Once used as an infirmary for wounded Civil War soldiers, a conch house in Key West, Florida, offers healing of another sort as a cottage retreat. (The conch shell, which used to wash up on Florida beaches in great numbers, gave its name to the Caribbean-style wooden dwellings that were built in Key West when islanders first settled in the town a century ago.) It's

The "lounge," like the rest of the cottage, is free of fuss and pretension. White, blue, and the natural shades of wood and wicker dominate the seaside palette, and a porthole-style mirror brings it all into focus.

129

a mind-cleansing refuge that makes no demands whatsoever," says Antony Childs, a Washington, D.C., interior designer, of a house where an exotic setting dominates the scheme. "The lack of decoration was intentional," he says. "Down here I want to focus on being outdoors." He used wash-and-wear cotton fabrics and kept windows free of curtains. The pine interior walls are bare except for a series of forty pencil drawings commissioned from his artist friend, Stephen Sidelinger, to evoke the music of Cole Porter, an elegant musical message in abstract black and white.

LEFT: *Six of the drawings from the Cole Porter series evoke two of the cottages muses: elegant music and the sea.*

LEFT: *A pair of iron beds, re-claimed with a coat of black paint, are turned out in summer linens.*

LEFT: *A newly made mirror from Ireland, inlaid with cobalt-blue and milk-white glass, reflects light from a pair of jug lamps.*
RIGHT: *The faux bamboo bookcase shows off Fiesta ware and sponge-ware in different shades of blue.*

In the living room, wicker furniture is generously proportioned for serious lounging. The French rattan pedestal table with intricate marquetry dates from 1870, about the time the house was built.

LEFT AND OPPOSITE ABOVE: *The dining pavilion functions as a room "with all the walls exploded out." A movable serving table finds many uses in the pavilion area.*

OPPOSITE BELOW: *In a town where space is always at a premium, the pint-size swimming pool is an oasis in cottage life. This one was trimmed in black and white to repeat a favorite color scheme in the house.*

OPPOSITE FAR RIGHT: *Tiles made in Cuba (and original to the cottage) pave the front entrance. An Adirondack chair adapts well to a Southern setting.*

LEFT: *A single tropical blossom suits a small cottage better than a large arrangement.*

COLLECTORS' RETREAT

The Berkshires cottage where Peri Wolfman and her photographer husband, Charley Gold, spend their weekends year-round is set among farmers' fields and two grand old red barns. "The property dictated what we should and shouldn't do when we moved in," says Peri. "It was a working farmhouse, built around 1900. We wanted to hold on to its integrity, so we kept it plain and simple, just as we imagine the original farm family might have furnished it." Peri filled the rooms with natural and painted pine, farm furniture, and her trademark white china and linens from Wolfman•Gold & Good Company, her home-furnishings shop in New

A New England farmhouse in the Berkshires embodies the timeless qualities of a rural cottage with its screened-in porch and a handsome picket fence. Here, a birdhouse with its own in-law apartment, flowers from the cutting garden, and a collection of child's and doll chairs are right at home.

York City. "White helps simplify my life and creates a serene place to live. For the country," she observes, "I warmed up the pure look with rustic painted pine pieces I found locally." Small stools and benches and the yard-sale glider that now graces the screened-in porch are all well suited to the cottage scale of the farmhouse.

When Peri and Charley, inveterate collectors, can't find a place for a newly purchased treasure, they set it out in one of the barns, which, as a result, are gradually filling up. A prize find that did not end up in the barn is the French baker's table in the kitchen. Peri says, "I think we bought this house so I'd finally have a place to put it." Spoken like a true collector.

ABOVE: *Crisp white trim draws attention to restored outbuildings, while the fence keeps pests and pets out of the vegetable patch and perennial border.* OPPOSITE: *A white-walled kitchen is the showcase for an eminently practical marble-topped French baker's table. Peri Wolfman added a shelf below for hard-to-store cooking utensils and serving platters.*

LEFT: *The round slat-top table, built by a local carpenter, allows cottage-style entertaining: in this case, salade Niçoise made with vegetables fresh from the garden, enjoyed in a room with a view.*

RIGHT AND FAR RIGHT: *Charley Gold, a gardener, is a passionate collector of old tools; Peri Wolfman specializes in rustic finds such as the twig armchair.*

OPPOSITE: *A glider from the 1940s looks up-to-date with fresh paint and new vinyl-coated cushions. The rocking chair and farm stools were located in the Berkshires.*

140

ABOVE: *The bathroom is cleverly constructed from two adjoining closets.* RIGHT: *Pale blues, lacy whites, and natural pine are the bedroom's dominant colors. In the hallway beyond, a collection of child's chairs hangs over a miniature seating group.*

NEW MOORINGS

That a shingled boathouse from a turn-of-the-century seaside estate could be transformed into the quintessential summer cottage came as no surprise to fashion stylist Barbara Dente. In Pennsylvania, where she spent family vacations as a child, a boathouse has the same rustic chic and modest scale as a lakeside cottage. Before renovation, the cottage stored boats in two slips. The original sliding doors are intact

In the era when summer guests often arrived by water, distinctive railings, columns, and windows were de rigueur on the boathouses of country estates.

145

and in use on the lower level, where the living room and kitchen are now located. The small upper level, once living quarters for the custodian, serves as the bedroom. There is rich architectural character

LEFT: *Flooring was added to the original slips to create an all-purpose room on the first level of the boathouse. The original doors are attractive open or closed.*

ABOVE: *White paint unites a miscellany of indoor and outdoor furniture from the 1950s.*

LEFT AND BELOW: *A bare painted floor epitomizes the sweep-out-on-Sunday-night appeal of cottage life, where humble Queen Anne's lace makes a dramatic floral display and a dog named Star has permission to seek any resting space.*

OPPOSITE AND LEFT: *The bedroom on the upper level of the boathouse gains a zesty cottage character from its painted pink ceiling and painted blue floor.* BELOW: *In keeping with the owner's Scandinavian roots, the boathouse/cottage has been pared to the bones and its wainscoted walls are kept uncluttered.*

in the shingle siding, porch pillars and rail, and the octagonal window. Inside, the walls and a pleasant miscellany of functional furniture are all painted white. The effect pleases Barbara. "I don't like a lot of clutter around me," she says. "Here, views of greenery, blue skies, and water are all the decoration I need. When I moved in, all I brought was my set of white linens."

LIGHT CONSTRUCTION

Light is really the principal color in this cottage," says Richard Martino, an art director who brought his sense of graphic design to refurbishing what was "a beach cottage so grim and dark it felt more like a cabin in the woods." Richard removed the dark stain from the soft pine floors, replaced a clunky mantel, and ripped out beams to open up the house to its rafters. He painted walls and woodwork a creamy white and added French doors, multipane windows,

'New Dawn' roses in pale shades are all the ornamentation needed in this spare but beautiful home. Shingles replace the original thatched roof, and simplicity of furnishings, inside and out, is a virtue. (PHOTO LEFT: CHRIS MEAD)

and skylights. "Natural light moves through the house now," he explains. Rather than tackle the house a room at a time, "a red room here, a patterned room there," Richard treated the entire house as if it were a single space, keeping everything clean and simple. "This way, I can take things from one room and move them to another," he says. "I like to change things around often, anyway, and I didn't want a lot of distractions inside." In the true spirit of cottage gardening, he planted roses all along the front of the house. He was astonished when the vines "shot up like Jack's beanstalk, six feet in one summer." His cabin in the woods became a sunny, rose-covered cottage a lot sooner than he had expected.

ABOVE: *A pine mirror in the living room reflects favorably on a neat row of trim topiaries and the mantel display on the opposite wall.*

LEFT: *French doors, multipane windows, and skylights ensure a constant stream of natural light into the cottage. Pine floorboards, the Eames chair, and the wide-board English pine table have natural warmth.*

OPPOSITE: *Lounge chairs at poolside flank an oversize flowerpot.*

A weather vane on the warpath, a set of boccie balls, and a pair of baby's first shoes make a curious still life on the mantel in a living room given a summer look with potted trees, fresh flowers, and a sisal rug.

ABOVE: *In a reading alcove, a reproduction sleigh bed dressed in white is joined by two modern classics, a Tizio table lamp and a Charles Eames laminated birch potato-chip chair from the 1950s. The kilim rug introduces one of the few patterned elements into the house.*

ABOVE LEFT: *Plumped-up pillows on the banquette in the living room.* ABOVE: *In the bedroom, white walls make a suitable backdrop for photography by Bruce Weber.* LEFT: *A pine armoire and a wire birdcage.* RIGHT: *A working weekend in cottage surroundings.*

In emphasizing simplicity, intimacy, and relaxation, cottages often inspire their owners to celebrate their colorful—sometimes eccentric—tastes. Quirky little buildings themselves, cottages accept with open arms the nonconformist's penchant for unexpected juxtapositions and brash colors, patterns, and textures. In some cottages, sophistication and wit underlie collections as varied as flea-market finds of retro furniture or primitive folk art from the villages of Guatemala. In other cottages, spirited originality creates the illusion of another time entirely, as otherwise mundane possessions are used to give the home as spirited a character as the person who inhabits it. Eclectic they may be, but these dwellings, like all true cottages, are unpretentious, comfortable, fun, and endearing.

LATIN
LODGINGS

Mario Montes takes pride in bringing the color-ful furniture and crafts of the mountain villages in his native Guatemala to his shop in East Hampton, New York. The remarkable artistry of the Indian crafts guilds in this Central American country is world renowned. Mario was even happier to introduce some of the rustic works he collects into the dollhouse-size cottage he acquired for a year-round residence. This former laundress's cottage, its tiny 660-square-foot interior cobbled together out of scraps of mis-

The traditional dove of peace (an old copper weather vane mounted on driftwood), sets the tone in a cottage where the colors and crafts of two proud cultures exist in harmony.

matched lumber, turned out to be an ideal blank canvas, as many simple spaces are. "Because I was on a budget, the ideas applied to turning the cottage into a home had to do with making it comfortable, livable, and, most of all, pleasant to be in," explains Mario.

Built in the 1930s, this stucco cottage—with tiny windows and peaked rooflines—is straight out of a Grimm fairy tale. The interiors, however, hadn't been spruced up since the 1950s, so some overhauling

ABOVE: *An old butcher-shop sign lends a playful note in the kitchen. The l930s cabinets were stripped and hand-rubbed with turquoise paint; doors were removed to show off prized vessels in daily use.* RIGHT: *A pair of New England jugs provides a homely counterpoint to a bowl sculpted and painted by Long Island artist Diane Mayo.*

ABOVE: *Pillows on the wicker love seat are covered with fabrics woven by Guatemalan Indians in intricate ikat design. The side table with its lizard head is an* *adult version of traditional animal-motif furniture. Made of cedro, a native wood of Guatemala, it was once used for public ceremonies.*

was in order. Mario stripped the woodwork, rag-painted the kitchen cabinets for a textured effect (and to disguise that they had been built of three kinds of wood), and removed most of the doors to eliminate the rabbit-warren effect. Then he added color to the walls, until, over time, the rooms took on the atmosphere of summer.

The most important addition to the cottage was the warm, distinctive ethnic flavor imparted by Mario's collection of furniture, textiles, and pottery by primitive Guatemalan, African, and North American folk artists.

A wooden blanket trunk made in Nahuala, Guatemala, "the village of carpenters," is inscribed with images of everyday local sights.

OPPOSITE; *Oak surrounds of doors and windows were stripped and finished with various paints.* ABOVE: *A cedro bench with native weavings—and hotel dishes.*

LEFT: *A collection of flowerpots made by the McCoy pottery works in the 1950s occupies a shelf above a daybed made up with a Pendleton blanket and Guatemalan pillows.*
ABOVE: *In a bedroom where the wood relief of Washington never sleeps, a Guatemalan headdress adorns an American country cupboard.*

167

COTTAGE IN TECHNICOLOR

Only in the city where Technicolor was made famous could a cottage painted eighteen colors and surrounded with hundreds of cacti be a welcome part of the neighborhood. "You couldn't get away with this anywhere except Los Angeles," says designer and artist Laurie Warner, who shares her kaleidoscopic quarters on a hillside overlooking the Sunset Strip with her filmmaker husband, Edward Garrick. The couple modified their 1950s standard-issue California ranch into an "eclectic canyon cottage." "We appreciate Baccarat crystal, but we love to collect colorful fabrics, folk art, rustic furniture, and 'outsider art.'"

A California version of the vine-covered English cottage greets visitors with cacti in all shapes and sizes and folk art from around the world. The leaves in the living room—landscape paintings by Chicago artist Carl Keeler—are the backdrop for an antique horn chair and candelabrum.

LEFT: *Native American jewelry has a natural roost on a horn knickknack tree and a chunk of coral reef.* BELOW: *Glass panes permit light into the dining area, where a carved bull's head with a feather headdress presides as a colorful folk trophy. The floor lamp is a cactus spine with stretched rawhide shade.*

ABOVE: *The linoleum-art floor in the office makes an eye-popping combination with the barrel cactus armchair made by Laurie Warner. Crafted of birch plywood and painted with acrylics, Laurie's fanciful furniture brings "the shape, color, and humor of cactus to our canyon cottage."*

ROSE COTTAGE

The "Little Switzerland" region of Arkansas's Ozark Mountains boasts a surprising range of Victorian hotels and guesthouses, none more romantic than the Rose Cottage of Rosemari Agostini and her husband, Doug Marsden, in Eureka Springs. "The guesthouse really is one big nook now," says Rosemari, but when she and Doug bought it, it was a cramped maze of tiny rooms. "We tore down every wall in the place to make cozy alcove spaces and spent two years burning off decades of exterior paint," recalls the Dallas-based designer. The couple repainted the house board by board in soft pinks, whites, and grays to give it an authentic look of faded roses.

Like the painted floors and other whimsical details inside, a dark and mossy bulwark of stone serves up a fairy-tale vision of cottage life. The fieldstone was painstakingly gathered from the Ozarks countryside and fashioned into a wall, with the biggest stones serving as garden steps.

PRECEDING PAGES: *In a room that says, "Salome Slept Here," old chintz fabrics, floral hooked rugs, and lace tablecloths cast a romantic spell. Doug Marsden's hand-made molding echoes the shell pattern found in the curtains separating sitting room from bedroom.* ABOVE: *Farm chairs in ruffles, a delicate herbal sampler, and a bay-window banquette atumble with pillows make for a room with a rosy and blithe spirit.* RIGHT: *A multiple family birdhouse has a place of honor in the garden.*

ABOVE RIGHT: *In the attic bed-room, flowers and ribbons ap-pliquéd on lace provide a veil of privacy in a tiny space.*
RIGHT: *On the porch, a tree trunk becomes a table with the addition of a glass top.*

TROPICAL PARADISE

For novelist David Kaufelt and his wife, Lynn, the old wooden cottage with its roof of seven gables and multiporch façade is a marriage of Victorian formality and contemporary technology, "a blissful union we call Trop Tech," says David. The cottage stands in Key West's charming Old Town, where the houses reveal the influences of the Bahamas, New England, and New Orleans: "Tin roofs, porches, cupolas, working shutters, revolving fans, gingerbread—Americana with an eccentric, even perverse, twist," notes David. When the Kaufelts bought the house, it was totally unlivable. "We discovered what realtors truly mean when they wax ecstatic over 'dream houses,'" David recalls. Built in 1907, the cottage was the creation of a car-

Located in the oldest neighborhood in the island city of Key West, an idiosyncratic 1907 cottage with an abundance of gingerbread and other romantic touches is the home of a novelist and his family.

LEFT: *A painting by Beth Nablo and a diminutive chair found in a second-hand store stand out in the white-floored, wainscoted center hall.* RIGHT: *A newel, hand-fashioned by the cottage's builder, steps into the future with stair treads painted turquoise. The table comes from East India.*

LEFT: *A patented oil-paint procedure requiring seventeen coats to achieve its yellowy parchment texture, seems made to order for Sugar Rae, the Labrador retriever. The mirror is of modern Italian design.*

penter-architect who designed the Durry mansion, also in Key West, for the first Florida millionaire, and built this cottage nearby for himself.

An eminently sensible living plan coupled with "the flights of architectural whimsy old Mr. Kennedy indulged himself in," David notes, made the house salvageable, albeit in need of modern upgrades to the kitchen and termite-eaten beams. Today he remains spellbound by the romance of his "little mansion."

ABOVE: *In the bathroom tucked under the eaves, the mirror is cut to follow the sloping ceiling.*

ABOVE: *On the second floor, a cedar-lined window seat solves storage needs as well as providing a comfortable place to relax and read.*

RIGHT: *Tucked under gables, the master bedroom has traditional Key West wooden walls, ceiling, and floor, all painted white.*

ABOVE: *Punctuated by skylights and soaring ceilings, the master bedroom is a favorite haven for Sugar Rae. An overstuffed rocker from the 1930s, found at a yard sale, is newly hip after having been upholstered in a jolting turquoise fabric.*

RETRO COUNTRY

It was the old porcelain kitchen sink that won me over," recalls Ellen O'Neill about how she came to rent the blue-shingled cottage with its tiny white porch. "I liked its straightforward character and that no one had tried to improve or replace it." Unlike other houses in the village of Sag Harbor, carefully restored to reflect the area's colorful whaling heritage, Ellen's rental retained the modest character of the worker's cottage it once was. "Fussy Victorian doesn't appeal to me," says Ellen, who responded to the fact that "the moldings were all there and the floors have a little lean to them." Rickety, not precious, is her preference for cottage furniture. "My friends kid me that they're never

Time appears to have stood still in this Victorian cottage, built in 1900 as housing for employees of the Bulova Watch Company. It's a cottage with the heart of an old-fashioned homemaker.

BELOW: *"An elephant going to a birth-day party in a pink tutu"* is the way *Ellen O'Neill describes the slipcovered chair in a patchwork of gingham and stripes. Pillows soften a willow rocker, and blue-and-white quilts bring country freshness to a cast-off sofa.*

RIGHT: *A cottage kitchen displays its collection of chipped china and Aunt Marion's Franciscan ware on shelves over the original porcelain sink. The slat-back chair, newly painted a 1940s green, once sat in a grade-school classroom. The vintage tea towel on a hook continues the period theme.* BELOW RIGHT: *In a hearts-and-flowers bedroom, the innocent charm of the 1940s is recalled in a bedside table and a matched set of polished cotton daybed spreads.*

ABOVE: *The colorful and shapely discards of previous generations are put to good use by a cottager who draws on old furnishings and fashions to add reasonably priced personality to a rental.* OPPOSITE: *A Depression-era starburst-pattern quilt and a 1940s floral spread double up on the painted iron bed bought for twenty dollars at an antiques fair. Plaid curtains contribute to the overall retro character of the cottage.*

sure it's safe to sit down when they come for a visit." But Ellen, who works as a home-furnishings stylist for Ralph Lauren, does wonders with things that wobble. For a few dollars she bought a shabby sofa at a local yard sale. "I took it home, covered it with a painter's drop cloth, and then threw some quilts over it," says Ellen, a true believer in the virtues of improvisation. "I've always liked the way farm families patch tablecloths with fabric that isn't quite the same but 'close enough.'"

Ellen's recent passion for fashions and furnishings of the 1940s and 1950s informs the cottage with a mischievous and winning style. Above all, her decorating message is about having fun with the past.

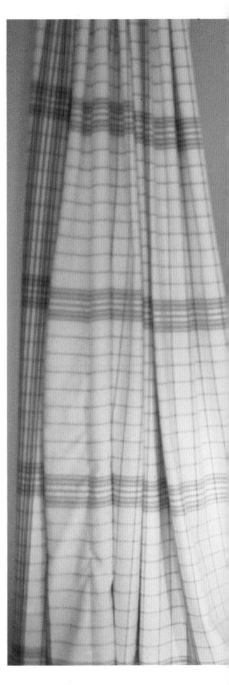

A COTTAGE HANDBOOK

A COTTAGE HANDBOOK

· · · · ·

Cottage Living

By definition, cottages are small, but they are often happily so. Intimate and carefree, they offer everything needed for work and play but few of the extra spaces that inspire those of us who are pack rats to save the unnecessary, keep the unwanted, and collect the unimaginable.

Perhaps the most important rule of cottage living is: Keep it simple. The owners and their guests spend most of their time outside anyway, so forget about tabletop vignettes that need constant dusting or landmark floors that need polishing. Instead, devote your efforts to creating friendly porches and patios and streamlining the passages between inside and outside, and save the grandeur for another kind of home.

Cottages often lend themselves to a nostalgic style, whether it's the humble-yet-romantic rose-covered look of 19th-century rural England, or the post–World War II "first home" feeling of our own parents' and grandparents'

houses (in fact, much of the housing that sprouted all over America in the late 1940s and early 1950s had the same limited spaces and need for charm as our present-day cottages). Some

of the practical and decorative tricks of earlier times can help us make our own cottages more lively and livable, from folding racks for dish towels to lace curtains that soften windows to farm baskets that hold firewood.

Whether you have lived in your cottage for ages or are just now moving in, this is the time to make a fresh inventory of your possessions. Earmark unneeded furnishings, accessories, and old clothing for

storage or a garage sale. The ideal is to live only with objects that are practical or attractive (or both).

Try to imagine every space in your cottage as it relates to your life there. If you typically entertain just two or three guests at a time, you may not need that heavy sofa; a wicker love seat and a pair of chairs recruited into service for dinner will do the job and save you space. If your cottage is by the sea, borrow practicality from shipbuilders: Invest in built-in drawers and cupboards, and install shelves under stairs, between eaves, and along the entry hall.

As you itemize and eliminate, however, don't throw out the favorite things that will lend the transforming magic of personality to your cottage. You will need welcoming places to sit and watch the sunset or to read a book, and you will need beautiful objects, colors, and the pleasures of nature in every room of the cottage.

A COTTAGE HANDBOOK

· · · · ·

Instead of giving up decorative objects, figure out how you can make them serve a purpose in your cottage. A pitcher can adorn a mantel, serve lemonade, or hold a dozen No. 2 pencils. My grandmother never owned a proper vase; heirloom pitchers made the best containers for her garden flowers.

We often love objects for their practicality as much as for their beauty. To me, being able to handle favorite objects again and again as I use them is what gives them the power to please.

A Cottage Notebook
Even for those of us who decorate for a living, it's often hard

to visualize exactly what a particular fabric or piece of furniture will mean in a room. One of the tricks of the trade is to collect tangible evidence of the ideas that interest us. Showrooms, museums, house-and-garden tours, catalogs, magazines, books, historic buildings, and the homes of friends all are invaluable resources.

I tear out pages from magazines, make color copies from books, and write down my thoughts in red Magic Marker on the pages of my secret weapon, the notebook. My favorite notebook is spiral-bound—it stays flat when I open it, and I can tape clippings directly onto the pages. (Some people prefer a notebook with a pocket for swatches and paint chips.) I divide my cottage notebook into sections according to rooms (kitchen, bedroom, bath, porch, living room) and general categories (color, light, storage, garden ideas, and so on). Be sure to sketch floor plans, with at least approximate measure-

ments, for each room in your cottage at the front of its notebook section. You'll be surprised

how helpful these notes and pictures will be when you sit down with a contractor or head for the flea market.

Cottage Basics
The best time to analyze the floor plan, working parts, and general décor of a cottage is when it is empty.

In order for the cottage to feel open, with rooms flowing naturally into one another, it may be desirable to eliminate some unnecessary doors or tear out walls that chop up the inte-

A COTTAGE HANDBOOK

· · · · ·

rior space. Unlike a large house, a cottage does not grant us the luxury of assigning a single function to each room, or of turning over part of a room to mere decoration.

Create short passages rather than long hallways to connect rooms, and use every opportunity to create nooks and alcoves. Make the most of windows, doorways, and other openings. These help to provide views from room to room, intensifying the sense of the cottage as one intimate space.

Now is also the time to consider adding windows, skylights (see page 202, "The Cottage Bath"), or dormers if the cottage needs more natural light or more headroom. Multipane windows are prettier to look at, more pleasing to look through, and let in a softer, more indirect light than picture windows.

A window seat, a perch ideally suited to cottage life, can be installed at a relatively low cost beside a dormer or bay window, giving you valuable extra storage in the bargain.

As you plan your cottage, make sure you note the passage of the sun over the house. Try to situate such areas as the breakfast nook or work studio with a southern exposure, granting

· · · · ·

COTTAGE STYLES AT A GLANCE
Here's a short list for giving your cottage a distinctive character.

COTSWOLD COTTAGE
Botanical prints, slipcovered furniture, wicker and rattan, stripped pine, flowered English china, paisley throws

FARMHOUSE COTTAGE
Baskets, milk-painted furniture, primitive portraits, ticking, quilts, folk-art signs

PROVENÇAL COTTAGE
Faïence, rush-seat furniture, French blue and mustard yellow, printed fabric from the south of France

ADIRONDACK COTTAGE
Stoneware, twig furniture, peeled logs, wildlife trophies, buffalo-check

fabric, Beacon blankets, fish and duck decoys, old National Geographic *magazines, vintage photographs*

WILD WEST COTTAGE
Navaho blankets, tin lamp shades with cowboy cutouts, cowhide rugs, log beds, leather chairs, branding-iron candles, fireplace tools

MAINE COTTAGE
Twig curtain rods, rattan furniture, fishing rods and wicker creels, striped awning fabric, sailboat models, shells and beach glass, old postcards, straw hats

195

them the most sunlight. Wake up naturally with the sun by choosing a room on the east side of the cottage as your bedroom.

When the walls in the cottage pose a decorating problem, I have found that the easiest initial solution is to paint them all white. Leave trims natural or paint them glossy white. You can avoid the antiseptic look by blending Benjamin Moore's standard Decorator White with their Linen White. The result will be a uniform interior that gives you a free hand in furnishing. Later, after you've lived in the cottage and know better what you want from your space, you can introduce pattern and color. Richard Martino's method of treating his entire cottage (pages 150–157) as a single room helped him to feel instantly at home. Since cottages are often summer or second homes, time for redecorating is often short. Once again, simplicity is the answer.

If the cottage has sound hardwood floors, it may be a good idea to refinish them now, before furniture and traffic arrive (to avoid that glossy bowling-alley look, make sure the floors are finished with a flat polyurethane). Vintage cottage kitchens often come with linoleum from outer space, but a dated kitchen floor *can* be salvaged: Paint it a solid color, in a checkerboard pattern, or with a stenciled design, then add an overcoat of poly to seal.

Furnishing the Cottage

The cottage is a more forgiving residence than a Georgian Colonial or an English manor house. It accepts a surprisingly wide range of furniture and accoutrements. That is one reason why my friends who are accomplished flea-market shoppers find it so easy to fill out their cottages so quickly and confidently.

A medley of unmatched seating, for example, can work in a cottage. A soft sink-into-it sofa, some straight chairs, a couple of benches and stools, the odd club chair or wing chair, and a wicker or rattan love seat can be brought together in a pleas-

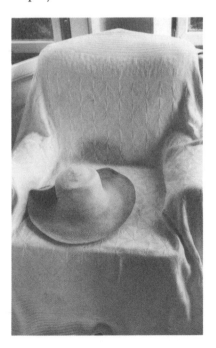

ing circle around the hearth or out on the porch. The variety of styles and sizes offers everyone a comfortable place to sit. (Unlike socks, there's no such thing as a one-size-fits-all chair or sofa.)

Slipcovers, originally used to cover the furniture of summer houses, are never out of place in the cottage. Less formal than upholstered furniture, slipcovered pieces have the added advantage of concealing a multitude of sins of taste and condition. A ragtag sofa discovered at the secondhand store becomes a princely addition to the living room when fitted with a few yards of attractive fabric.

For summer, use washable materials such as natural duck, ticking, and white denim. For winter, a set made up in a floral or classic tartan or paisley pattern provides a completely different look that is just as livable and appropriate.

Improvise with slipcovers, as my friend Emelie Tolley (pages 46–51) did. To create an instant sofa, she covered an ordinary

twin bed with removable wraparound bed covers, using as bolsters oversize pillows encased in lacy antique shams. When a guest needs a place to sleep, Emelie simply removes the slipcover.

Temporary slipcovers can even transform hideous summer-rental furniture. With a few yards of inexpensive duck and a handful of upholsterer's T-pins, you can achieve a fitted look and hide that tacky couch or chair. It's a trick I learned when I started producing decorating features for magazines, and I have found it invaluable in

decorating my summer cottages.

The cottage's setting often dictates the style in which it is got up. Along the Eastern Seaboard, cottagers draw on Yankee, nautical, and farming traditions. In California, inspiration for interiors often comes from such diverse sources as the Spanish Colonial period, the cowboy West, and Golden Age Hollywood. In the Florida Keys, the tropical colors and patterns of the Caribbean show up in most conch cottages. And along a river in Arkansas, a cottage's trappings might be the gear of fishing or boating.

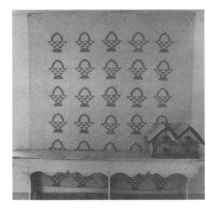

But it's your cottage, and it has to express your personal style. After years of collecting for myself and for others, I am convinced that each of us is his or her own best curator. When it comes to bringing personality into the cottage, trust your tastes and brainstorms, your whims and impulses.

The cottage is the perfect venue for personal expression. Undoubtedly, there are treasured family photos and other mementos that deserve a place of honor there, on one corner of a wall or atop a chest or table. Whether collectors are serious or casual, the cottage is the place to share one's love of handcrafts, folk art, dishware, bottles, baskets, quilts, or, in the case of Lys Marigold (pages 18–23), dog portraits.

A playful spirit is found in many cottages. In a cottage, you can let down your guard and leave the decorating dos and don'ts for others to bite their nails over.

Cottage Light
The unforgettable "rosy" atmosphere in many cottages is literally just that—a space suffused with the warmth of pink light. Light tinged with pink (or red or yellow) is perceived as warm and inviting to the human eye, while light tinged with blue, gray, or green is seen as cold.

The illumination of a room is a combination of the sunshine coming in through windows, the light provided by fixtures, and reflections of interior colors and surfaces. The trick is to experiment with color schemes until the room seems to bask in a warm glow. Trust your own eye and instincts in working to achieve a warm ambience in the cottage; that radiance can make all the difference.

· · · · ·

USEFUL COTTAGE ACCESSORIES

- *platters*
- *bowls*
- *lamps*
- *baskets*
- *candlesticks*
- *pitchers*
- *quilts, coverlets, mattress ticking, Marseilles spreads, homespun*
- *divided boxes*
- *old books*
- *picture frames*
- *throw rugs*
- *peg racks*

The cottage garden contributes to light in its own fashion. When window boxes are filled with flowers, and portals and windows have roses, clematis, or bougainvillea growing around them, the light coming into the cottage is rich, warm, and natural, not harsh or flat.

In the evening, use a combination of firelight and lamplight to infuse the cottage with a cozy atmosphere. A wood fire on a chilly evening, a few kerosene lanterns, and an assortment of candles on the mantel or a table add a flickering warmth and glow. I like to use small table lamps and floor lamps to create intimate niches bathed in their own pools of light. A hanging light fixture over the dining table brings supper guests together and fosters conversation with a sense of intimacy.

Collecting for the Cottage

Moving into a cottage offers many of us a chance to do what we enjoy most—shopping for bargains and treasures. It's amazing how much charm and character can be added to a cottage, without breaking the bank, just by knowing where to shop and what to look for. My favorite resources are flea markets, tag sales, junk shops, country auctions, and antiques stores.

Small antiques have been essential to my cottage decorating style (see pages 78–91). Rustic benches, stacked one on another, make a useful bookcase that can be disassembled when extra seating is required. Look for tiny chairs and stools to use as quaint side tables. Old firkins will hold magazines or store wood for the fireplace. Divided boxes make good desk organizers or silverware totes. For your outdoor entertaining, a bottle carrier can serve as a portable bar, a condiment holder, or loaded with bottles full of freshly cut flowers, as an attractive centerpiece.

Keep alert for baskets in all shapes and sizes to help you keep your cottage neat and

organized. Baskets have always been a hallmark of country style, and they have a valuable role in the cottage, too. Farm baskets,

· · · · ·

ACCESSORY OF THE MONTH
In preparation for the move to the cottage, write a list of accessories you are missing. Make up a budget to purchase at least one of the desired items per month for as long as it takes to round out your collection.

English wicker baskets, gardener's trugs, Shaker baskets, wire egg baskets, gathering baskets, picnic hampers, and small woven baskets can all be used to store the things that tend to create clutter and disorder, such as cassettes and CDs, family snapshots, games and puzzles, fireplace kindling, magazines, and paperbacks.

Old bottles and pitchers are always in abundance at neighborhood tag sales. Collect them in your favorite colors and use them as vases throughout the cottage, individually on windowsills and tabletops, or massed in groups and filled with wildflowers from the meadow or blooms from the garden. Meticulously engineered floral displays may work in grand dining rooms, but small, informal bouquets are usually most at home in a cottage.

Vintage textiles and linens can always be found on the flea-market circuit, and I like to stockpile them for many uses. White tablecloths can be trans-

formed into curtains by running a seam at the top and inserting an adjustable tension rod. You can make similar use of pretty cotton dish towels by sewing them together.

To make charming covers for throw pillows, look for old quilt tops, men's white linen handkerchiefs, scarves, or bandannas, and sew them together in pleasing patterns. Floral curtain panels made in the 1930s and 1940s happen to be my passion.

I recycle them as window valances or to cover chair cushions and pillows.

Everything I collect is used in the daily life of the cottage, whether it's a modest milk bottle or a valuable family heirloom. My English platters and bowls and my textiles—quilts, Marseilles spreads, and Pendleton and Beacon camp blankets—are stored on open shelves or in cupboards with see-through doors, so that I can enjoy them even when I'm not using them. There's no fun in having things if you hide them away for special occasions, because those are too few and far between.

The Cottage Kitchen

Traditionally, the cottage kitchen is a communal place, casual and full of life. It is neither overmeticulous nor isolated. It is more like a real farmhouse kitchen or the bustling keeping room of a family in Colonial times. I collect small still lifes of food—strawberries, watermelons, and the like—and hang them randomly in the kitchen to make it cheerful and homey.

The best cottage kitchen is as informal as it is practical. Rather than installing a permanent work island, use an old harvest table as a prep counter. Look for one with a trestle base so that you can easily add a lower shelf, as Peri Wolfman did in her cottage (pages 136–143), to store essential cooking equipment like the blender and the food processor, as well as mixing bowls, baskets, rolling pins, and chopping blocks.

An old painted cupboard with drawers can be most useful and at the same time lend its warm character to the kitchen.

Cupboards with glass-paneled doors let you see at a glance where everything is.

If there is room for a rocker or any comfortable old chair, you will be surprised at how much use it gets. Its inviting presence helps to ensure that the cook isn't left alone.

Storage is always a challenge in a cottage kitchen, but over the years I've discovered a few tried-and-true solutions that seem to work in every circumstance. Open shelves mounted on decorative wood brackets can hold a pantry's worth of glasses, dishware, platters, and other necessities. A wooden plate rack is wonderful for storing—and showing off—your colorful heirloom china. Take advantage of that space over a doorway to install yet another shelf. There you can keep accessible less-used but still necessary things. Sometimes, I prop a painting up there or line up a row of earthenware jugs and pitchers.

Anyone who has ever visited a Shaker museum knows how clever and efficient peg racks are as a storage solution. In a cottage kitchen, a long peg rack is handy for stowing your slickers, bomber jackets, and baseball caps. Smaller racks should be hung in strategic locations on walls and over counters to hold sets of important keys, workhorse utensils such as graters, measuring spoons, cookie cutters, dish towels, and pot holders, or a prized collection of antique kitchen tools.

Find a wooden barrel or large

ceramic crock to use as your waste container, using it with disposable plastic or paper sacks. If it doesn't come with a cover, have a wooden one made to keep a lid on smells. (I store my supply of replacement bags in the bottom of the trash bin, under the bag in use. That way, when it's time to take out the garbage, my new bag is there at the ready.)

If there are any dark corners or counter areas in the cottage kitchen, look for one of the small track-lighting systems now available. They are easy to install, and you can put them where you need them. A small conventional table lamp with a fabric-covered shade casts a friendly light on the worktable or on a countertop.

The Cottage Bath

The perfect cottage bathroom has the comforts of a spa and the serenity of a woodland pool. Given its crucial therapeutic role, the bathroom in a cottage deserves thought and attention. Cottages seem to lend themselves to old-fashioned bathing. If there is room, an oversize bathtub is a worthwhile luxury. Even a large shower stall can be added to most bathrooms. One friend of mine cleverly con-verted two closets in her cottage into separate lavatories, one for the shower and one for the privy. An outdoor shower, even if the plumbing is rustic, is a must for any beach or lakeside cottage. For its fragrance, plant clumps of moisture-loving mint at the periphery of your outdoor shower.

White tile on the floor and halfway up the walls of a bath-room, with the rest of the wall area painted white, creates the illusion of more space (some-thing most cottages benefit from in *any* of their rooms), and pro-vides a neutral background for the decoration you may want to introduce. Enhance the cottage character by replacing a stan-dard medicine cabinet with a wooden cupboard or a framed mirror. A small chest of drawers and a tiny chair or stool help to furnish the room with agreeable storage and utility. A peg rack on one wall and hooks on the back of the door can be used for robes, towels, and sleeping gar-ments. (In my bathroom I have

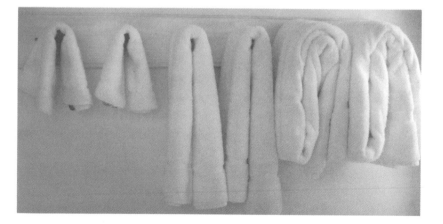

a small peg rack for my Indian jewelry, headbands, and lace collars—a convenient storage place for a splash of exotica.)

If your bathroom has access to the roof, consider installing a skylight over the bathing area. Without interfering with your privacy, this window on the sky will bring the natural world into the room and make the cleansing ritual even more soothing.

The Porch

In this country, the first front porches appeared in the South; their popularity quickly spread as people all over discovered the versatility of this "outdoor room." The porch is the sine qua non of cottage life, offering a place to watch the world go by, a rainy-day shelter for fun and games, and a sensual locale for entertaining when the scent of roses or wisteria is upon the air.

The porch's location in relation to the sun dictates its appropriate use (a deep front porch facing south will receive the most visitors). Striped awnings help to make a sunny porch cooler and are a handsome element in their own right. If the porch is on the shady side of the cottage, treat it as your refuge on sweltering days and a sleeping porch by night. In most parts of the country, *any* porch should be screened in if you want to use it during the evening hours in bug season.

Furnish your porch with pieces that can stand up to weather. Willow and wicker chairs, hickory rockers, twig furniture, hammocks, and old-fashioned gliders are traditional, but an old church pew or the flowery chaise longue your aunt gave you might fit just as well. Native American rugs and blankets always seem to fit on the rustic porch, adding cheerful colors and designs that blend in because they were inspired by the natural world.

To make the porch even more habitable, set out an old floor lamp along with kerosene lanterns and citronella candles (to keep mosquitoes at bay). Old painted benches as side tables and coffee tables are also useful. And don't overlook the house wall that forms the back of the porch. Here you might hang a sign hand-painted with the name of your cottage, or install a rack to hold fly rods, tennis and badminton rackets, and foul-weather gear.

A COTTAGE HANDBOOK

· · · · ·

The Cottage Garden

The humble cottage garden predates all of the elaborate garden types we know from the 18th and 19th centuries. It began as a small plot a step away from the cottage of a farm worker or tradesman, where herbs, vegetables, and flowers were raised for family use, and beauty was just a by-product of the garden's practical function. In both 18th-century England and Colonial America, such gardens flourished.

"Unselfconsciousness" is the essential spirit of these gardens, writes Patricia Thorpe in *America's Cottage Gardens.* That quality, along with sheer ebullience, has characterized most of the cottage gardens I have visited, in keeping with the spirit of the cottage itself. Cottage gardens are less structured than traditional row or border gardens. Their romantic appeal lies in irregular rather than symmetrical design, unruly rather than manicured appearance, and an individualistic mix of herbs, bulbs, wildflowers, vegetables, vines, annuals, and perennials.

Even when located in the same region, no two cottage gardens are ever the same. Every cottage owner has a unique gardening personality, and a garden should reflect personal enthusiasms just as it suits the growing requirements of a particular cimate and soil.

· · · · ·

SOME FAVORITE OLD-FASHIONED COTTAGE FLOWERS

Anemones

Asters

Baby's breath

Bee balm

Bleeding hearts

Calendula

Carnations

Clematis

Cosmos

Cranesbill geraniums

Daffodils

Daisies

Delphiniums

Forget-me-nots

Heliotropes

Irises

Hollyhocks

Lamb's ears

Lavenders

Lilacs (Syringa varieties)

Lilies of the valley

Nicotianas

Pansies

Peonies

Phlox

Pinks (Dianthus)

Poppies

Primroses

Rosemary

Roses

Southernwood

Stocks

Sweet rocket

Sweet william

Thyme

Violets

A COTTAGE HANDBOOK

· · · · ·

I like to "furnish" my cottage garden, and I believe that light-hearted little additions give the plantings more personality and make the garden more fun to

look at and more inviting to visit. Utilitarian objects that help to humanize (and humor-ize) the cottage garden are skeps, sundials, weather vanes, bird-baths, fanciful birdhouses, and garden signs.

Pathways to and through the garden lead the way for visiting friends and should be made from natural materials such as fieldstone, pebbles, crushed oyster shells, old weathered bricks, or even heart-shaped stepping stones.

When a garden is fully or partly enclosed, the surrounding

fence determines its character. I'm always looking for antique gates and fences; classic white-washed pickets, twig wattle, or simple dry-laid native stone can also provide an appropriate rustic embrace for the cottage garden.

I love the garden gate. It embodies the sentiment and poetry that the cottage garden is all about. A pergola planted with flowering vines or covered with climbing roses makes an impressive entry; a more rustic gate might be fashioned from timber brought back from the woods or driftwood collected on the beach. For the Bicentennial, I added a carved and painted early American wooden flag to my picket-fence gate.

· · · · ·

FORAGING FOR THE COTTAGE

It's easy and fun to bring elements of the natural world into the cottage. A hike through the woods or a walk on the beach provides the occasion for scouting in the wild for all manner of objects.

A bird's nest or a hornet's nest (uninhabited) is an authentic and appealing reminder of the wild kingdom atop a mantelpiece or on the bookshelf with your nature titles.

A sturdy broken tree limb can serve as a rustic curtain rod or shower-curtain hanger.

Seashells and driftwood belong in every beach cottage. Half fill the glass base of your kerosene lantern with colorful small shells or pieces of beach glass.

Bleached animal skulls found during hikes, bird feathers, milkpods, thistle, or specimen butterflies arranged on a pinning board can all be incorporated into your cottage décor as a tribute to natural science and to the naturalist's collecting impulse.

A COTTAGE HANDBOOK

· · · · ·

Cottagekeeping

The Cost of Cleanness, published in 1908, calculated how long it took to clean an eight-room house: twenty-seven hours a week. But that was the era of coal dust and oil lamps and mud from unpaved sidewalks and streets. One pundit wrote of spring cleaning, "It breaks women's backs and causes men to break the Ten Commandments." Emily Dickinson was even more succinct, commenting in one spring diary entry: "House being cleaned—I prefer pestilence."

Fortunately, today's cottage, by its very nature, is much easier to look after than yesterday's Victorian house. (And truth be told, we are probably more tolerant of imperfection than wealthy Victorians—who, after all, had maids and gardeners to help with the work.) In fact, one of the appeals of cottage living today is its practicality and convenience.

To keep my cottage fresh and in tune with the seasons, I take out my checklists and roll up my sleeves for three major refurbishings each year. My "commandments" should, of course, be adapted to your cottage, but the general idea is to be organized of plan and ruthless of execution.

SPRING

Pick a sunny day to throw open windows. Take down curtains and strip bed linens, then wash them and hang them outside to dry in the fresh air. When they're damp but not wet, bring them inside to iron.

Wash down the cottage walls with a liquid cleanser, such as Murphy Oil Soap.

Sweep out the house from one end to the other. Rent a commercial waxer to polish the wooden floors.

Clean out closets, installing cedar liners to store your woolens. (Every spring, I buy new white plastic hangers for all my summer things—it's a small expenditure, and it makes me feel good.)

Clean out kitchen cupboards and shelves and reline them with fresh paper.

Take down all your books from their shelves, dust them, and replace them systematically.

Hose down your porch and garden furniture, baskets, window boxes, and bikes.

Straighten out the garden shed, cleaning and reorganizing tools and equipment, and make up a shopping list for the garden center.

Plan your early plantings in the garden and for your window boxes and other containers.

Make up a list of the fix-its and other chores that have accumulated over the winter—paint touch-ups, screen and window repairs, mending loose steps and wobbly chairs, etc.

SUMMER

Pull up dark rugs and leave floors bare, or replace them with rag rugs, striped dhurries, or sea-grass mats.

Remove curtains and valances and leave windows uncovered where privacy is not a concern. In bedrooms and bathrooms, use half curtains or just hang pairs of lace panels.

Put summer slipcovers on the furniture. Replace the covers on your winter throw pillows with a lighter floral pattern.

Dress beds in light layers of white—white sheets and shams, a Marseilles or piqué spread, and white cotton blankets.

Add surprise to the fireplace by laying birch logs, a mass of jumbo pinecones, or a decorative birdhouse—something attractive to fill the hearth for the summer months.

To keep the cottage in a summer mood, display kitchen baskets and bowls filled with seasonal produce, put out vases of cut flowers daily, and fill a blue-and-white platter with fun family snapshots from last summer.

FALL

Restore the cottage's cozy look by adding layers of colorful blankets and wool throws to beds and upholstered chairs and sofas.

Change pillow covers, bringing back your suedes and homespuns, plaids and dark florals.

Put down your oriental, Navaho, or other woolen rugs, and restore winter treatments to the windows.

Put new wicks in kerosene lamps, check your candle supply, and lay in kindling and firewood for the hearth.

Set out bowls of fresh spicy potpourri, fragrant herbal topiaries, and dried flower arrangements.

For vivid color throughout the winter months, set up a schedule now for forcing bulbs in pretty bowls and dishes.

Recommended Reading

Alexander, Christopher. *The Pattern Language.* New York: Oxford University Press, 1977.

Baisly, Clair. *Cape Cod Architecture.* Orleans, Massachusetts: Parnassus Imprints, 1989.

Downing, A. J. *The Architecture of Country Houses.* New York: Dover Publications, 1969.

Downing, A. J. *Victorian Cottage Residences.* New York: Dover Publications, 1981.

Gilborn, Craig. *Adirondack Furniture.* New York: Harry N. Abrams, 1987.

Kidder, Tracy. *House.* Boston: Houghton Mifflin, 1985.

McAlester, Virginia and Lee. *A Field Guide to American Houses.* New York: Alfred A. Knopf, 1984.

Rybczynski, Witold. *Home: A Short History of an Idea.* New York: Viking, 1986.

Thorpe, Patricia. *America's Cottage Gardens.* New York: Random House, 1990.

INDEX

· · · · ·